The DreamBuilding Diary

YOUR PERSONAL JOURNEY TO CREATING AND
LIVING THE LIFE OF YOUR DREAMS

Kiylise M. Lowe, MS.

Founder & Chief Dream Engineer of
The DreamBuilding Co.

Copyright © 2020 Kiylise M. Lowe
All rights reserved. This book or any portion thereof may not be reproduced or used in any manner whatsoever without the publisher's expressed written permission except for the use of brief quotations in a book review.
ISBN: 978-0-578-70219-3

Dedication

I dedicate this book to my loved ones who are no longer present in this physical realm. I continually live the life I see when I close my eyes. When times become challenging or difficult, the memories we have shared ignite me to keep building and dreaming.

I think of you often.

the dreambuilding diary

Acknowledgments

Acknowledgments and Gratitude to the following:

- My Hubs: Osiris
- My OG Dream Team: (KSC & The Team)
- My Heartbeats: Brittany, Michael, Aamir, & Braylin
- My Soul Tribe Sisters & Mindset Coach MMJ
- My Dreamers: Erika, Cheyenne, DaJanai, Demia, Honoré, & JeQuilla

Your outpouring of love and support pulled me through this crazy ride numerous times. You have influenced the production of this magic in one way or another.

Lets Build!

dreamer

Contents

Welcome — Pg. #1
→ Suggestions for getting started.

Evolution — Pg. #5
→ Inspiration station.

Chapter 1: Envision the Vision — Pg. #18

Chapter 2: Evaluate Plans and Goals — Pg. #54

Chapter 3: Establish an Identity — Pg. #94

Chapter 4: Engage Others — Pg. #129

Chapter 5: Execute the Dream/ Experience the Outcomes — Pg. #156

This Book Belongs To:

Name: _____

Email Address: _____

Social Media Handle(s): _____

Hello Dreamer,

*W*elcome to your Personal Journey of building, creating, and living a life you love and see when you close your eyes. This diary will hold and possess all of your dreams that consistently replay in your mind. It will also keep the things you have yet to think through and develop fully. It's an actionable blueprint for the life you are destined to lead. You will begin thought organizing, analyzing, and learning more about what you truly want in your dream life. The inner workings of the diary are the things that you explore and discover. The actual workings are the things you plan and prepare— here is where your ideas transform and become a workbook, a workbook/diary/toolkit if you will. You will explore how passion, purpose, and power all work together to build and launch your dream life. The 5 **E**ssentials highlighted throughout this book are the building blocks I used to launch many things in my dream life. Your Dream Journey starter kit includes: **Envisioning the Vision, Evaluating Plans & Goals, Establishing an Identity, Engaging Others, Executing the Dream/Experiencing the Outcomes**. You will dive deep and engineer a real plan for success along with many other tidbits, tools, and resources. Each chapter includes an *inspiration station* section with short reads and articles about dreambuilding, as well as a *notes* section for you to reflect and challenge yourself.

Suggestions for Getting Started:

- **Favorite Writing Utensil:** I have this pen, you know, the really nice ball pens that you get from work, a restaurant (accidentally appropriated after signing for your bill), or the one you splurged and actually decided to buy. It's the ink pen that makes your handwriting magical. You'll need your favorite magical writing utensil and a safe space to keep it.

- **Planner/Calendar:** Having a personal planner or calendar on hand is super important because as you embark on this dreambuilding journey, you'll need to dedicate time every day, every weekend, or every month to work on building your dream life. If you're just starting and don't have a whole lot of time, try dedicating at least 30 minutes per day to envisioning the life you desire. The more you practice, the easier it becomes. Be sure to power off your phone, mentally log off of social media and spend intentional time working on this.

- **Accountability Partner:** Everyone needs a little motivation. I'm challenging you to find at least one accountability partner. It can be a close friend, family member, or mentor. I'm also only one email away if you need me. Empower your "AP" to check-in on your progress. Routine check-ins help to keep you on task. I don't want you to set your dreams aside.

- **Fav Place:** Find your favorite inspirational spot and stake out your very own workspace. If you're a spatial person like me, you'll need some elbow room to brainstorm and work your entire process. Doodling is an all-time favorite of mine as I brain dump. Make sure your working space works for you.

- **Dig deep with honesty:** Truly knowing where you are will only take you where you desire to go. Do not worry about who or what you see around you; just remember this is your journey and your time. Be honest and open. Transparency is key to building your dream.

- *Enjoy!*

Welcome | Suggestions for Getting Started

Start where you are,

Use what you have,

Do what you can.

—Arthur Ashe

Evolution

Evolution

I began this journey many, many moons ago. I took a huge leap of faith and reached high for the stars. I was so fed up with desiring more out of my life. I was so sick and tired of waiting for something magical to happen for me. I was tired of sitting like a mysterious unicorn on my own planet just staring at my watch. To solve my problem, I immersed myself in connecting the various dots of my life. The things that brought me great joy deserved to be praised by none other than me. I decided to start fangirling over myself and all the remarkable things I was already contributing to my life. I began shifting my focus from that inner burning desire of wanting so much more to celebrating my wins and what I already had. I tapped into the core of who I am. I shifted my thinking and changed my mindset. Once I began my entrepreneurial journey, I found myself peddling quite fast. I was fearlessly throwing myself out there as a creator and new entrepreneur. I knew my gifts would be beneficial for others because I had already explored the things lacking in the lives of the youth and women I talked to and worked with daily. We all shared a commonality, and I simply wanted to provide the help I couldn't find. The support that I wished would have magically appeared before I found myself pushed to the edge of stagnation and fear. I decided to leap, and while that sounds easier said than done, it wasn't the leap that ultimately caused me to act. Leaping is something that becomes a continual process when you're a dreamer. Leaping doesn't just occur once, and boom, all things are answered. You'll continue to leap (and leap some more), but it's what you do with those amazing jumps that matter. I needed a thought-organizer to help me create an actionable blueprint for my dream life. To solve my problem, I created one that worked for me. I wanted to organize my thoughts, appeal to my learning style, and brainstorm more intentionally. I created a series of tools that helped me solve my problem, and then replicated the process and those tools in my first version of The DreamBuilding Diary. I was brand spanking new to the entire world of books and publishing (which is always a continuous journey). I spent countless nights researching and learning what I needed to do to make my dream of helping others become a reality. I sacrificed many nights of sleep and found myself knee-deep in the world of YouTube and online articles. Fast-forward four years later, and I could literally write a dissertation on my evolution. Taking a leap of faith to reframe my thinking has blessed my life in so many ways. Creating tools to organize my thoughts have blessed my mental health in so many ways. Blessed. Blessed for sure. In the first version of The DreamBuilding Diary, I wrote all about my pain points, the very thing that drew in so many new dreamers because they could relate to my struggle. I now had a tool that could assist with the first steps toward living more abundantly. My struggle was simply being fearful and non-actionable. The action piece is critical to success. I am that person that came out of the womb dreaming about possibilities but putting action behind those dreams is why I now write from a different perspective. Let me recap where my leap has landed me.

Officially, my leap began when I launched my business 8StorySocial. The entire idea behind it was birthed many, many moons ago in a college apartment, but 2016 was my year of action. I soon ventured on to also launch my *Because Dreams Win* blog, where I shared weekly posts about the tips and tricks of living the life you see when you close your eyes (you'll find many in the inspiration station section of this book). I eventually rebranded 8StorySocial to The DreamBuilding Company because I quickly discovered that you should not grow an old idea into a new need. *Message!* The DreamBuilding Co. was chosen for dreamers who need the tools to get started dream living and doing. I began working with a select group of women providing what I call dream engineering. We would literally talk on the phone and complete DreamBuilding Diary worksheets together. These were the same thought-organizing worksheets I created for myself that I was now using to help others. I've even shared really intense text messaging convos with some of my dreamers. We would solve their problems and organize their thoughts via text as needed. I was just using various vehicles to get the work done. Those relationships only ignited my fire to continue this life connectivity thing amongst others. I saw the need for dreamers who were simply "stuck" and void of self-care. That later developed into a more intimate space for women to share their stories and escape from their day to day lives with other like-minded women. The Dream (R) Retreat was birthed and held to highlight the complexities of women who may never become the face of an empowerment event. Women who are rich in life experiences and have no desire to be in huge arenas. They simply found value in intimately sharing their stories with others. I created that platform to celebrate them with the goal of helping implant the practice of "retreat" into their dream lives. Each retreat focused on a different set of "R" themes: relax, renew, reconnect, and refresh, relate, release, etc. With such a high demand to continue the conversations of sharing stories and what I crowned in my blog series as "Tea (spilling the downfalls) & Triumph (sharing the wins)," I launched my next project Dining with Dreams. Women came together to break bread, continue spilling tea and triumph, and ultimately share resources to help move their lives toward their goals. As I continually found women reaching out via email, reading blog posts, commenting on IG posts, and more, I knew these gatherings and discussions were missing links from all of our adolescent years. The forums for women to convene were just lacking, so the conversations organically continued. My lifelong passion and profession of working in the youth development field and alongside young people birthed The DreamBuilding Academy. I used the same practices from the DreamBuilding Diary to help teens gain confidence and grow leadership skills. I brought in other powerful voices to share their experiences with teens and to model dream living. I've shared firsthand conversations with youth about who their role models are, and they certainly don't look anything like the powerhouse women I know. I was so excited to pilot the academy for teen girls. Two years later and I have been fortunate to see a wonderful return on the investment in young authors and designers' lives. It's a really phenomenal feeling to see young people empowered because they're just so absolutely brilliant! I could go on and on about how my leap of action continually grew in other areas of dream living (Creative Concierge, Speaking Engagements, Workshop Facilitation, etc.). This recap is not to brag about what I've accomplished but more to demonstrate how shifting my thinking allowed my actions to follow suit in my dream living. I'm still on fire and ready to turn up the heat by sharing my growth. I've been super stretched, and my creative hands have dabbled in spaces I thought I didn't belong. The growth I've experienced has brought me back to these pages. I said this before, and it still stands true: stop searching for a status-update-worthy life and instead embrace a praise-update-worthy life filled with crushing your goals and living your dreams. Doors will begin to open. It doesn't matter who you are and how disadvantaged you think you may be. You have to plan and prepare for the life you want. Take it from me; I believed I was the least qualified, non-advantageous, young, black woman from an impoverished, "no-parent" household. I simply got fed up with that belief and took action. It wasn't easy because I've been fed up many times before, but this time it was truly the approach (action-centered is real y'all!). I also discovered that I am highly qualified for this position I've created for myself despite all of those aforementioned intersectionality's. I developed tools that allowed me to act on my passion, purpose, and power. I want you to do the same. Guess what! Your time is now. This workbook is your blueprint, your plan, and your chance. You have entered the DreamBuilding Headquarters. The 5 Essential principles are organized for you to experience within these pages. I am confident that you will gain great takeaways, and I simply cannot wait for you to win! I can't wait to read about your glow up.

Now lets get started.

Dream Journey Starter Kit

ENVISION THE VISION
EVALUATE PLANS & GOALS
ESTABLISH AN IDENTITY
ENGAGE OTHERS
EXECUTE & EXPERIENCE THE DREAM

Inspirtation Station

Playing with Fire

*F*ear can feel like playing with fire. I've been there and done that. Fear kept me stuck for quite some time. Take notes on the following feelings fear can leave you with and what helped me to overcome them. *Lets Play.*

What fear does…

CRIPPLING- fear will cripple your ability to do. Fear is the fire that will leave you stuck. You can get so stuck in your own insecurities and thoughts of judgment from others that you just avoid moving altogether. Everything inside of you desires for something, while fear and doubt literally cripple your ability to move.

FEELING LEFT BEHIND- once you are crippled by fear, you may notice that you are feeling left behind. Oftentimes you may sit back and watch others live out their dreams. Fear will allow life to continually move forward regardless of where you are. It doesn't care that you're left behind and stuck, others are just living while you're fearful. Goals are still being accomplished while you're contemplating.

VISION BLOCKING- fear will block the good images of what living your best life looks like. You see fire by way of disappointment, confusion, and lack of confidence. You'll begin thinking that there is no way you can do the things you want when your vision is blocked.

How I overcame it...

FAILING- dreams aren't perfect; failure is real. Once I decided fear would never hold me hostage again, I failed. Womp, Womp! I honestly believe that failing was pivotal for me. It discouraged me, but it also gave me the fight to never be defeated. I believe failure is absolutely necessary for growth.

SHARING- I could have sat on that failure like it didn't happen to me but the moment I opened my mouth to share that it did, doors magically opened. Share your story, your shortcomings, and everything in between. This is what separates your journey from others. Simply live in your truth and help others along the way.

TRYING AGAIN- I could have taken my blows and let fear continue to cripple me. I decided to try again and again and again, and I'm still trying. I literally attack my goals. I create them, and I give them my all. There's a lesson and a blessing in everything. Keep trying.

*I*f you can relate to the fear of even getting started, we will get a cool handle on these fiery hurdles. We'll talk about how to cope with a life that's not all cupcakes and sprinkles. I promise.

What has fear held up in your life?

Share your story:

Welcome | Evolution

Self-Agreement

Throughout this journey, I agree to:
- Be open and transparent about my goals.
- Be intentional when organizing my thoughts.
- Show myself grace when I get confused, flustered, or discouraged by life happening to and around me.
- Trust the Process, Be Fearless & Celebrate my Wins!

Dear Self,
Throughout this dreambuilding journey, I also agree to:

Chapter 1

Envision The Vision

Envision the Vision

Welcome to Chapter 1: Envision the Vision.

I absolutely believe you have a bold vision. I can just feel it. I appreciate that you've started this journey, and I want to share how important it is to organize your thoughts and create an action plan for moving your dream forward. In this chapter, I will walk you through some discovery exercises that will help you paint the big picture. I enjoy seeing the big picture, so I can drill down on smaller tasks with my vision always leading.

I introduced my **P**assion, **P**urpose and **P**ower formula in the first version of this book, and I still live by it. Once you connect your passion to your purpose, you will begin operating in your power. This chapter will inspire you to think about those things. Your goals, your vision, your bucket list, your hobbies— they all matter. As you curate and create a life you see when you close your eyes, alignment will be extremely important in doing so. Begin by painting the big picture that informs how and why you'll build your dream.

Let's Build.

Chapter 1: Envision the Vision

You are the recipient of GREAT! You have crushed your goals, and the world is ready to celebrate your hard work and dedication. This is your moment. As you receive this **lifetime achievement award**, you now have the opportunity to reflect on the journey that got you here. Let's begin with the end in mind.

Here's a brief example of mine:
Imagine me on a huge stage, glamorously dolled up with tears wailed and waiting for release: "I'm so honored to be here today to receive this award. My success and work as a Dream Engineer have been so fruitful. From the lives I've impacted to the products I've produced, I'm so thankful to live this dream. None of this would have been possible without those who have believed in me (holds award higher in the air). I want to first thank God for his grace and mercy. I want to thank my Grandmother for planting and cultivating the seed of creativity by giving me the autonomy to dream, imagine, and create as an adolescent, and I want to thank my dreamers who have trusted me with helping them to build". Ok, I could go on and on, but I now pass the mic to you.

Reflection Questions

1. What do you want to be known for and who have you impacted?
2. Who has helped you get to this moment and who has been your biggest supporter(s) throughout your journey?

Take a moment to outline your speech here:

a.

b.

c.

d.

e.

Notes:

Acceptance Speech

The Dream Building Diary | your personal journey to creating and living the life of your dreams

"Begin with the End in Mind"

-Stephan Covey

Timeline Goals

Take a moment to map out specific benchmark goals in your life:

5 Years From Now	
5 Months From Now	
5 Weeks From Now	
5 Days From Now	
5 Hours From Now	

Timeline Goals

Take a moment to map out specific benchmark goals in your life:

10 Years From Now	
10 Months From Now	
10 Weeks From Now	
10 Days From Now	
Hours From Now	

ENJOY EVERY MOMENT

Chapter 1: Envision the Vision

Power in Words

Power **w**ords are the words that matter to you most. They're the words that manifest in your life and bring meaning to your existence without explanation. Your word bank is forever evolving so feel free to frequently revisit with new deposits. Jot down words associated with what you feel about your dream life. If you ever get stuck during a writing prompt or exploratory activity, remember your power words reside here. *Example: travel, joy, fashion, light, love, vibrations, stardust, magic, etc.*

Top 10 Things I Desire to Accomplish/ My Bucket List

1.

2.

3.

4.

5.

6.

7.

8.

9.

10.

Bucket List Sorting

Now that you've created your top 10 items you want to accomplish as you live a life you dream of, it's time to sort and categorize where these things fit. Categorize a total number for each in the descriptors below. This will help position priority on the things you can reach for first. Example: 3 are travel-related, 2 are personal passions, etc.

_____is/are socially related and apply to friendships, relationships, or things involving other people.

_____is/are business/career or financially related and apply to things I want for my life.

_____is/are health/beauty related and apply to how I want to feel or look in my life.

_____is/are spiritual/soul related and apply to how I want to manifest and spend time within.

_____is/are adventurous or travel-related and apply to experiences I wish to explore and have.

_____is/are personal passions and apply to the things that may not be in my wheelhouse but interest me anyway.

_____is/are _____ .

Dream Bucket List

Fill your bucket

A Day in the Dream Life Of...

Each day, I wake up at_____am/pm. I get my great start by preparing to conquer my goals. Once I'm all prepped and prepared I usually _____ or _____. I spend the next_____hour(s) doing_____. When I am feeling hungry and in need of fuel, my go-to meal is _____. While eating, I would love to enjoy a casual conversation with _____. I would enjoy that time most because it gives me a chance to _____. My absolute favorite part of my day is when I can _____. This is what brings me great joy and helps me to realize that I'm living my dream life. Once I've conquered my daily goals, I usually_____. I enjoy this time doing _____. As I find myself needing or desiring more fuel and/or energy I try to indulge in _____. Each day may be a different adventure, but I am most happy and fulfilled when I have an

opportunity to _____. This is just one day lived in my dream life. In a *limitless* world I would _____.
I absolutely look forward to taking this leap and launch into what is next for my dream life.

Signed,
A Determined DreamBuilder

Thought Corner:

_____

_____

_____

_____

_____

_____

_____

_____

_____

_____

My Dream, My Vision

*U*nleash your creativity right here on these pages. This is your chance to create a vision board that highlights the things you envision for your life. Use markers, colored pencils, stickers, magazine cut-outs, and more to create a visual representation of what you will manifest in your life. Feel free to make one for different areas of your life (*business, social, familial, etc.*).

The Dream Building Diary | your personal journey to creating and living the life of your dreams

Vision Board

Chapter 1: Envision the Vision

Vision Board

Vision Board

Quick Write Moment

*T*ypically, we spend the least amount of time planning a life with no barriers. We often plan around financial limitations, resources, ability, and talent. During this quick write moment, jot down what a meaningful life with no limits really feels like for you. Focus on the vibe you want to manifest and the feeling you want to radiate to the world. What do you really want?

_____

_____

_____

_____

_____

_____

_____

_____

_____

_____

_____

_____

Passions X Hobbies X Dreams

Passions by Hobbies, by Dreams. What are you passionate about? What hobbies hold your attention? Your dream life should be filled with a great combination of both, that work for one another. Let's explore how they connect & align. If you have yet to land on something concrete, jot down aspiring passions (things that intrigue you and are important), and hobbies (things you love to do for pleasure & fulfillment):

Example: Passions

1. Writing
2. Taking Pictures
3. Home Décor

Example: Hobbies by Dreams

1. Blogger / Copywriter
2. Photography
3. Home Styling

Inspirtation

Station

DreamBuilding 101

Get Connected: Are you truly connected with like-minded people or just a bunch of cool acquaintances? Are you the only *"Aspiring"* individual within your circle? Are you sharing conversations regularly that help you grow? If these questions leave you pondering, then I charge you to seek out new circles now to begin your dreambuilding journey. No shade to your cool friends either, but we're talking about building a life we love. Begin with finding a support group that applies to your niche and where you can build a sense of community. Try finding groups on Facebook, Meetup, or Eventbrite. It could be as simple as a group for new moms, new entrepreneurs, or new interior designers (it's your pick). Join, connect, and take the leap! Grab your squad of like-minded people because trust me, they're out there, and they're already dreambuilding.

Get Hip: Have you done some preliminary research on your market? I recently heard someone say they wanted to start a book club. My response was, "Why?" I wanted to gain more information about their why while helping probe them to think deeper. Was it because they wished they already belonged to a book club, could it be just because it sounds fun and fulfilling? I wanted them to begin thinking of these questions in a way that would shape sustainability and momentum. That's exactly what I want you to do as well. Get hip to what is already happening around you. You must research your niche, your potential competitors, and your Why! Know your idea inside and out. You need to recreate a wheel with a twist so that you stand out in a room full of wheels.

Get Some Help: There is absolutely nothing that is out of your reach! I promise. If you want to start a company, you can. If you'd like to quit your job, you can. If you want to hop on a plane and see the world, you can. You can do all things (Philippians 4:13)! What you cannot do is: any of those things without being the best you. I preach about this all the time: make the investment in yourself and allow someone who has walked that path to equip you to do the same. Invest in coaching, a master class, or a webinar series. Get out there and continually develop yourself. There are tons of free and paid resources that will get you on track and leverage your potential.

Get Yourself Together: Speaking of developing yourself, don't forget about caring for yourself. Indulge in self-care. Take care of your body, mind, and spirit. Feed and water those things so they're good for you and continue to blossom. Take some **YOU** time and feel good. Healing is a huge part of any journey and as you build the life you see when you close your eyes, be sure to keep your sanity at the core of it all. Your dream life deserves the best version of **YOU**.

Get Your Goals In Order: One of my challenges was putting real action to my goals. I had a million things in my head that I wanted to accomplish. I didn't know where or how to begin. I just knew I wanted it. I needed to organize my thoughts and figure out a real actionable plan; I just needed order and balance. Use the activities in this book to prioritize and understand your goals. This is your journey and your mission to build. *You've Got This!*

Thought Corner:

_____

_____

_____

_____

_____

_____

_____

_____

_____

_____

Affirmation Boards + You

*Y*ou are *b*eautiful, *f*earless, *i*ntriguing, *a*mazing, and more, but of course, you already knew that. There were definitely moments in time when I knew those things about myself but didn't fully believe them. I want to share the magic that affirmation boards own and how they've fueled my life.

A few years ago I shared an intimate evening (until 4 am) with my best girlfriends creating our vision boards, and of course, immersed in girl talk. I thought about the vision board I created in 2014 (since this had become an annual practice for us). The entire board contained all quotes and affirmations and truly wasn't a typical vision board at all. There weren't any pictures on it, just magazine cut-outs of powerful sayings. As I now sat to do my vision board, I found myself doing the same exact thing. I was inclined to cut out words, sayings, and phrases like queen, strong is beautiful, boss, happy, etc. Affirming words that make me feel good and constantly remind me of who I am and what I possess. That affirmation board sat in a beautiful frame on a shelf in my office. Each morning I stared at those words and watched how they crept into my subconscious and psyche. I manifested those affirmations, and now when I see those words or think about the power I possess, I wholeheartedly believe it. I'm always reminded, and I want you to be reminded as well. *Lets Create.*

Chapter 1: Envision the Vision

DIY: Affirmation Boards

Materials:
- Grab a gang of magazines or computer printouts
- Scissors
- Glue sticks
- Poster Board or Cork Board
- Thumbtacks (if using a corkboard)
- Picture Frame or Adhesive for Hanging

Directions:

1) Cut out your favorite phrases, sayings, quotes, or words that represent you and make you feel affirmed and amazing

2) Just like a vision board, *design, create, frame,* and *hang*.

3) Recreate & Repeat as often as needed.

Affirmation: a statement that is declared to be true

Practices I use when creating my boards...

- Cover all the white space (that means filling my board corner to corner and leaving no small space behind).

- Frame my finished masterpiece using a decorative or plain frame that matches my home office or bedroom.

- Intentionally posting my framed masterpiece in a space that is visible. Make sure you are seeing your affirmation board and be reminded daily of the power you possess.

Hey Dreamer,

Do me a favor and email me a picture of your finished product to info@thedreambuildingco.com or tag me on IG or FB (@thedreambuildingco) and I'll be sure to feature it everywhere!

You're amazing.

I attract all good things

Dream Retreat Often

As much as I love a structured, planned, weekend retreat, I know my soul absolutely craves more frequent retreat vibes. To get clearer on my vision or even make space for new dreams, I often need a reset. I have charged myself with taking quarterly 1-day retreats, and now I pass the baton to you. The charge is yours to share. There are 6 important tips and tricks you need to include during your retreat to ensure you're planning it with intention and action.

Enrichment Activities

You'll need to include an enrichment activity that stimulates and sparks your mind. An example of an enrichment activity is finding a class to attend, such as Public Speaking Techniques, Real Instate Crash Course, Holistic Care, etc. Find a class that sparks interest for you. There are so many classes and activities you can find locally by using sites such as Eventbrite, Meetup, Groupon, or Facebook. If you can't find a local opportunity that piques your interest you may want to seek out a virtual offering. Using sites and apps like Peloton, Classpass, or Mind, Body, and Soul are also great alternatives to find new classes ranging from cycling to meditation. If that isn't your thing there are other trendy experiences you can try such as axe throwing, archery, or painting parties. Choose something you wouldn't normally do to create a new and meaningful experience for yourself. Did I ever tell you about the time I enrolled in a ballet class? *Epic Fail!* But hey, at least I tried! #rhythmlessMe

Intentional Activities

*I*ntention is what it's all about. What separates your 1-Day Retreat from any other date with yourself is the intention of your strategy. Be sure to plan intentional activities throughout your day. This should include scheduling time to enjoy your favorite meal. It can be breakfast, brunch, lunch, or dinner, but be sure to enjoy a wonderful meal that sparks joy inside of you. Be intentional about scheduling a relaxing activity like a bubble bath, massage, or pedicure. It's also imperative that you include something that serves as a treat to yourself. Treat yourself to shopping for something new (a splurge is ok), or maybe your favorite dessert, smoothie, or cocktail. #Cheers

Reflection Activity

*T*his final activity is most important to wrap up your retreat day. Be sure to plan some intentional time to reflect. You can plan a session to journal your thoughts, create a vision or affirmation board, plan your next four quarters or finish thought organizing in your DreamBuilding Diary. Whatever you choose to do, be sure to release anything that no longer serves you and plan ahead with realistic goals.

Take as many 1-Day Retreats as your heart desires.

1-Day Dream Retreat Checklist

Retreat Date: _____

[ ] **E**nrichment Activity: _____ Location: _____

[ ] **I**ntentional Activity: _____ Location: _____

[ ] Food that Brings You Joy: _____ Location: _____

[ ] Relaxation/Pampering: _____ Location: _____

[ ] **Other** (*Your Pick*): _____ Location: _____

[ ] **R**eflection Activity: _____ Location: _____

Planning Reminders:

Enriching: Try something mentally stimulating.

Intentional: Self-care practices (relaxation, joy sparking, etc.).

Reflective: Rid space of things that no longer serve you & immerse in thought.

Enjoy your recharge.

Notes:

Chapter 1 Recap

Chapter 1: Envision the Vision	
Acceptance Speech	Think ahead about how success will look for you.
Timeline Goals	Create a timeline: short term and long term goals.
Power in Words	Identify your power words.
Bucket List(s)	Explore things you aspire to accomplish.
Dream Libs	Take a look at a Day in Your Dream Life.
Vision Boards	Design a visual representation of your dream life.
Quick Write	Plan with no limitations.
Passions & Hobbies	Connect your passions and hobbies. (Where do you excel?)
Inspiration Station	Short Reads (Insights, Tips, etc.)
Notes	For you to create.

Evaluate Plans & Goals

Chapter 2

Evaluate

Chapter 2: The Process of Evaluating Your Plans and Goals

*H*ello Dreamer! You are now ready to move to the next step of this diary/workbook /toolkit. I hope you've gained clarity around the dream life you want to live. If you have, then you are exactly where you're supposed to be. It's time to <u>evaluate your vision</u>. What exactly does that mean? I'm glad you asked.

*I*n this next chapter, you are going to take the vision that you carved out and look at how your current resources, plans, and goals align. Don't forget when I say vision, I am referring to whatever dream goal you have in store. These next activities and tidbits will help you realize some of your current patterns and habits. You'll take a real look at your values, finances, and dream wish lists. You'll also work on my infamous dreambuilding formula. I've briefly talked about the concept of "investment in self," but you'll explore so much more of that in this chapter. This chapter serves as an introspective approach to understanding how your dream life will unfold. You've already laid the foundation for your vision, so let's continue to build upon it.

Visiting Your Values

The beautiful thing about your dream life is that it belongs to you. In fact, it doesn't have to look or feel like anyone else's. In a social media-driven society, we often feel success is measured by things others deem as important. I want you to ponder on that for a minute. People who don't know you, and who have never met you, basically get the opportunity to make you believe the narratives they tell. Nope. Nah. We're not doing that. Your dream life is YOUR dream. It consists of the things you think are incredible and fulfilling. It is a culmination of what your soul values in your life. Your internal conflict arises when your values aren't often shared collectively. You get confused with knowing if what you truly desire is what equates to success. I'm here to remind you, it is. Your values matter.

You may value traveling the world, starting a family, or loving your career and climbing a corporate ladder, which are all fine things to value. We're going to paint some very vivid pictures of your personal values embedded in your personal journey. It's similar to how we connected your hobbies and passions, but this time we're focusing on the things that you feel called to in whatever way that may be. My favorite part of understanding your values is understanding how our lives are so very different. We just value different things and that my friend is ok.

Thoughts on Values:

Visiting Values

*W*hat's your *W*hy? It's such a simple question but also one that is very loaded and can be challenging to answer. Just think of the thing that drives you. If passions are things that tug at our heartstrings, then think of values as the moral compass behind those. Now is your time to be honest about the things you value in your life. Someone interested in creating memories may be focused on living in the now, whereas a person who values securing their future may be focused on saving for later. Their *"Why"* all boils down to what's driving them. What's driving you?

Value: _____ Why: _____

Value: _____ Why: _____

Value: _____ Why: _____

Value: _____ Why: _____

Value: _____ Why: _____

Value: _____ Why: _____

Visiting Values

Example:

Environmental Sustainability	Carbon Footprint/ Recycling/Upcycling
Youth Development	Providing Resources/ Mentoring

Values:

The Formula

This formula serves as a pivotal foundation for dream living. Prioritize the things you're passionate about and unveil where your purpose and power connect. *[Passion: things you love; Purpose: things you're called to do; Power: the confidence you possess and the magic you create from connecting the two, your plan to live in your dream]*

List your top 3 below:

Passion:

Purpose:

Power:

Passion by Purpose by Power

My passion is _____

My purpose is _____

My power will be _____

Goals and Confidence

*T*hink about a time when you absolutely crushed one of your goals. When were you triumphant and able to celebrate your wins? Go ahead, you can smile as you reminisce. When I launched The DreamBuilding Academy, my goal was to help youth gain the confidence to build a dream goal, and the power to launch it. Confidence and power were the two things that illuminated my drive. Let's reflect on your moments now:

Goals I've conquered:

*C*apture a list of the things that worked well for you (i.e., planning, saving, mentorship, prioritizing, etc.)

_____

_____

_____

S.M.A.R.T.I.E.

Specific: What do you want to accomplish:

_____

Measurable: How will you measure your outcomes?

_____

Attainable: How is your goal within reach given your current load?

_____

Realistic: How is your goal relevant to your purpose in life?

_____

Timely: When will you have action steps completed? *(30, 60, 90 days)*

_____

Inclusive: Who has a seat at your dream table? Do you unintentionally exclude anyone?

_____

Equitable: What systems or barriers are you impacting with your goals?

_____

Commitments

What is currently on your plate? What commitments do you have in your life? What's something that has consumed your time? (work, family, hobbies, etc.)

- ○
- ○
- ○
- ○
- ○
- ○

Areas to Strengthen: Tools & Resources Needed:

Challenge: Name one thing you can commit to starting today to help you grow or balance your commitments?

Evaluate

Money Management | How are you currently spending your cash? This exercise is not quite a budget, but it's a great start at creating an outline for a budget. This process helps me to visualize if I am pouring my money into the right buckets. Sometimes I tend to drop the ball and a lavish dinner takes precedence to paying for ink for my printer. When I have these things written in plain sight, it becomes so much easier to manage.

Create a list of your current recurring purchases such as subscriptions, guilty pleasures, frequently purchased items, etc. These are things you can currently afford.

_____

_____

_____

_____

_____

_____

_____

_____

Evaluate

Things I desire to afford include:

Chapter 2: Evaluate Plans & Goals

Dream Budget

Income: _____ **Income Source(s):** _____

Housing	
Mortgage / Rent	
Electric + Gas Utilities	
Internet + Cable	
Water, Trash, Sewer	
Other:	
Monthly Living Expenses	
Groceries + Dining Out	
Gas	
Cell Phone/Wi-Fi/Cable	
Clothing/Beauty/Household	
Entertainment	
Childcare	
Spending Cash	
Other:	
Long-Term Expenses & Investments	
Auto Insurance	
Health Insurance	
Life Insurance	

Car Payment & Insurance	
Travel / Vacation Budget	
Gifts Budget	
Savings /Retirement	
Other:	
Monthly Summary	
Total Income	
Total Expenses	
Difference:	

Other:

Dream Budget

Take some time to budget other expenses you may have that are related to your business, hobby, travel, or some other passion:

Dream Life Fund

If you have money left over in your budget, what are you contributing to your dream life fund? Fill up your dream life jar with things you can begin purchasing or saving for [*i.e., crafting supplies, attending entrepreneurship workshops, traveling, etc.*]:

Investment

[in ˈves(t)mənt]: the action or process of investing money for profit or material result.

The most beneficial investment you can make is the investment in yourself. The investment that requires you to believe in YOU! To obtain the power of your passion and purpose, you're going to have to make deposits in your own bank. We all invest in ourselves in one way or another but in order to invest in your dream life, you're going to have to shift your mindset. You may even have to do some checks and balances and move things around in your life. I invested in my entrepreneurial journey by making those shifts in my life and in my finances. I joined coaching programs, paid for one-on-one calls, filled my calendar with weekly professional development, and even traveled for conferences. I simply shifted my budget of purchases I thought brought me joy and invested that money into growing me.

How can you invest in your dream? _____

What can you invest? _____

What are you willing to sacrifice? _____

What are some professional development opportunities that would greatly benefit you? _____

_____

_____

_____

Return on Investment

ROI (**Return on Investment**) measures the gain or loss generated on an **investment** relative to the amount of [money, time, effort, skill, pain, and devotion] invested.

Let's take a look at Returns. I'll map out how my return on investments look, and then you'll have an opportunity to do the same. You may also use this activity to goal set some returns that you want to manifest in your life.

Investment	Return
Education (college, post-graduate)	Knowledge, Degree, Higher Salary, Social Experiences, Lifelong Friendships
Owning a Pet	Unconditional Love, Companionship, Responsibility, Joy
Exercise & Fitness (Subscription)	Feeling Great, Physique Changes, Endurance, Health, Strength, Lifestyle
Dream Living	Purpose, Power, Happiness, Ability to Inspire Others, Legacy

Investment	Return

Your Return on Investment

*M*y greatest return on investment was becoming FEARLESS in my pursuit. I've become wiser, stronger, and more confident. The things that once scared me crazy, now excite me. I hold space for things that seem impossible. My return has been setting goals and crossing them off my list. It has been envisioning my dream life and then living it aloud. It's your turn to think about the times you've seen a great return on an investment in your own life. Write a story about that time and how it made you feel. Be sure to share what you sacrificed for your investment.

_____

_____

_____

_____

_____

_____

_____

_____

_____

_____

The Dream Building Diary | your personal journey to creating and living the life of your dreams

Toolkits & Resources

*H*ere are a few tools in my toolkit (past and current), and depending on your dream goals, some may be helpful for you. I want you to explore and research tools that align with your dream goals. Use this page to keep track of what they are and begin creating your very own toolkit:

Mindset Coach	www.monicamariejones.com
Group Coaching Program	www.thepowercollective.co
Website Hosting	www.wix.com, squarespace.com
Email & Document Filing	www.docs.google.com
Payment Processing	www.squareup.com
Invoicing	www. honeybook.com, paypal.com
Online Appointments	www.acuityscheduling.com, square.com
Design (& CCS)	www.canva.com, adobe.com
Project Management	www.trello.com
Print On Demand Merch	www.printful.com
Meetings | Courses | Calls	www.zoom.com, thinkific.com

Dream Goal #1 _____

Dream Goal #2 _____

Dream Goals #3 _____

The Dream Building Diary | your personal journey to creating and living the life of your dreams

ToolKit

Resource Name	Purpose	Website

Dream Goal Overview / Top 3

GOAL #1

Completion Date:

GOAL #2

Completion Date:

GOAL #3

Completion Date:

Evaluate Your Vision, Plans, & Goals Roadmap

What do you see for your life?
_____
_____

How is your dream aligned with your values?
_____
_____

How does your passion and purpose intersect?
_____
_____

What emotions do you feel when you look at the big picture of your dream?
_____
_____

How do you handle self-doubt and worry?
_____
_____

Who can you count on as you build this dream life?
_____
_____

What resources are available to and for you?
_____
_____

Inspirtation Station

Self-Investments & Deposits

*F*inancial investments are not the only deposits you should be making in your dream life. Have you made a necessary deposit in your personal or social bank? How are you currently investing in yourself? Here are 3 tips to ensure your dreams are lucrative.

Tip 1: *Mentally invest in avenues for advancement.*
I preach about Professional Development (PD) just because it's so bomb and a trend right now more than ever. With the popularity of podcasts, social media live streams, audiobooks, and other self-help platforms, PD is being thrown left to right. I'm an avid investor, but I want you to seriously consider next-level advancement. If the "free" information and resources are good, just imagine what paid services could offer. Now, I too have been on the skeptical side of if it's free and it's working, why pay? Or what if I pay and it's not that great? Listen, in order to live the life God has promised you, you're going to have to do some serious work, and because God is not mediocre, you can't just settle. I advise you to make financial investments into avenues for advancement. Consider joining a coaching program or mastermind group. Think of your dream life in HD. Next level status requires next level investing. It's all a matter of perspective, but the advancement opportunities I've paid for have truly taken me to higher heights in my thinking alone.

Tip 2: *Deposit into your social bank.*

Work. Work. Work. If you're anything like me, you know how DISCIPLINE plays a major role in making sure you don't solely work your life away. I literally can get on my computer and become a living zombie. I'm an ambivert, leaning a little more toward an extrovert, who lives for laughter. I absolutely make sure that I continually deposit moments that bring me joy into my social bank. Are you visiting or hanging out with friends regularly? Do you have standing dinner dates or happy hours? Are you traveling or partaking in other events that bring you joy? If the answer is no, you have to change that now. If those things don't speak to you, then just be sure to carve out time for the things that socially fill you up. Making time for Play is being super intentional about filling up your social bank with non-work-related things. I challenge you to begin by adding at least one monthly playdate to your calendar. I promise, it'll shift your energy and mindset.

Tip 3: *Physical Deposits Also Matter.*

This final step isn't all about fitness and working out. While that is certainly one of my core values, I do understand, *"it ain't for everybody."* Your physical transaction is simply about your confidence. It's how you rock it, how you wear it, and how it manifests opportunities for you. You have a light that deserves to shine, and your physical dwelling is the beholder. If it's physical fitness such as investing in a gym membership or walking the stairs instead of taking an elevator, allow your energy to be shifted by your body. If you need to wear a special color of lipstick or get a new hairstyle or haircut, do whatever you need to do to make you feel like the true boss you are. Invest in your confidence because after all, it belongs to you. Make the investment to feel better and to use your dwelling to radiate into the world. *You Got This!*

Notes:

_____

_____

_____

_____

_____

_____

_____

_____

_____

_____

Evaluate Your Evolution

3 Ways to embrace the *shift* in Your Dreams

As we talk about Evaluating Your Plans and Goals and truly connecting the things you desire, I want to let you in on something that is bound to occur during your journey. It's what others see as distractions that sometimes become pauses—it's called Evolution. It's the thing that occurs when you're stretched. I am an Evolution Queen. I've crowned myself, stepped out of my body, and observed my own process. I've literally looked at my mind and said, "What is really going on?" like seriously. Maybe your dream has shifted a bit. Maybe you're ready to start something new or something fresh. Nothing is wrong with you, trust me, I've been there thousands of times wondering, why is my mind shifting? Why am I inspired to do other things or to not see this thing through? It's simply called growth & evolution. We evolve as we learn and as we're exposed to new things. I had to learn how to manage those evolving moments.

Here are 3 things that worked best for me:

Write It Down. It feels awkward. Your mind may be all over the place. One of my best practices is carrying a notebook with me everywhere I go. It's a necessity. I planned my Dream Retreat from the backseat of my best friend's car as we drove up north for a weekend vacay. You never know when you're going to be inspired.

You may feel like you're losing focus but don't worry, we're all on a journey here. If you feel like you're all over the place, and simply don't know what to do then it might be wise to revisit your values. They certainly can change but we often forget to ask ourselves the most basic question of all: What do you want? Write down your current emotions and feelings and then answer the question. What do you want? If you don't know, continue on this dreambuilding journey to flesh out your thoughts and ideas.

Talk About It. Find one person you can share a real, and raw conversation with. If you don't have that person, don't forget I'm here for you (info@thedreambuildingco.com). You're going to realize that your evolution doesn't sound that crazy to others. Be sure you stand firm on it and share that with someone. We spend so much time bottling up our thoughts, our emotions, and our dreams. To truly live the life of your dreams you have to find people to share them with. You have to talk about what your plans are even if it's just to drive yourself out of doubt and worry. Talk about it with someone you trust and someone who will be honest with you. Someone who will listen attentively, give constructive criticism, and no matter what, still support you. If you don't have anyone to listen, we need to build your dream team. When I say find someone, I am not by any means referring to creating a status update, I am charging you to get on the phone or schedule a coffee date with another human being you know. Connect.

Pivot with a Plan. Pivoting in your dreams is natural. Think of major brands that have scaled, expanded, and pivoted their businesses. We wouldn't love Nike as much if they only stuck with selling sneakers. We all love gray Nike joggers (right)? You can pivot without fear. The fear that you're entering a new market, a new niche, and that your followers and supporters won't understand. If you're committed to doing your market research and figuring out a concrete strategy that supports your evolution, your fears will be no more. The goal is to create a plan. You're not Beyoncé, so you can't just drop a new biz on us and expect it to break the internet. We need a planned launch. We need a backstory, sales funnels, and all of that good stuff. Whatever your dream is and wherever you are with living it, evolution and growth are bound to happen, so be prepared to pivot with a plan.

Recap:

1. *Write it Down*

2. *Talk About It*

3. *Pivot with a Plan*

Tea & Triumph

*E*valuating plans and goals and assessing your vision is important because we're often told to just take the leap. While I'm all here for the leap, let's secure our landing so that the bounce-backs don't hurt that bad. I love this step because it forces us to make sure we're truly sure about our goals, our values, and our desires for dream living.

I created Tea & Triumph as an opportunity for individuals to share their amazing accomplishments (Triumph) but also to disclose some of their challenges (Tea). My goal is to continue the narrative that often leaves creatives feeling discouraged and alone. Life is real and mistakes happen. Sometimes after we leap, our landing is trash. We have to normalize the hardships so that we learn from the many lessons of pursuing the triumph. When I take time to evaluate my vision, I like to be 100% honest about challenges that may come or roadblocks that may arise. This series was created with that in mind. Here's a Tea & Triumph moment with none-other than your own Chief Dream Engineer (*me*):

A huge triumph in my life right now is managing and dealing with my grief. Despite all of the amazing things I do in my dream life, I'm still human. I experience the stages of grief on a daily basis, and as an adult, I have to adequately keep my grief in a manageable state. It's my triumph because I'm most proud of doing this work and securing my healing journey. My intrinsic motivation to want to be better, feel better, and do better has been all the push I've needed. It's such a huge triumph for me because I once was so afraid to tackle this area of my life. I'm a master at pushing through my pain and in the past three years, I've decided to take it all on. From grief groups to yoga, to journaling, to therapy, I'm trying. I'm winning. I'm triumphant.

*O*k, let me spill my tea. Tea is simply stating my truth and disclosing the not so pretty side of my "dream." As my business The DreamBuilding Company continues to grow and evolve, I have experienced my own pivot pains. Pivot pains come with growth. I offered a new service within my business and it was crafted out of a demand from clients who were ecstatic for this new offering from someone they trusted. I found this lucrative offering to keep me busy and oftentimes overwhelmed, but I just pressed through anyway. I was dead smack in the middle of planning my wedding, stressing over all of that stuff, and dealing with the unexpected passing of a very close loved one. There were some preliminary things I needed from my clients, but I failed to set those boundaries and systems in place prior to immersing in this offering. I felt burdened; like I had a job I dreaded. It got crazy. I'm saying all this to say that I evaluated what the heck I was going through, and I honestly felt like I failed the wonderful people who counted on my services. I was no good to them because I honestly never made my boundaries clear yet had a list of expectations of how we should be working together. I have learned that many entrepreneurs have experienced something similar. When I confided in a colleague about the experience, he reassured me that it happens to the best of us. I have chosen to allow that service to work for me (bring me joy), instead of the other way around. I honestly didn't expect to emotionally feel the way I did, but it happened, and I'm moving forward with a new vision. *My tea is now lukewarm.*

Extra Extra: Catch Up With Me:

(Some of my Favs):

TV show(s): Insecure (HBO), Love Life (HBO Max), Grace & Frankie (Netflix), 9-1-1 (Fox), The Morning Show (Apple TV),

Podcasts: Ted Talk Daily (every single day), Dissect Podcast, Girl Trek Black History Month Bootcamp, This Week in Culture Podcast

Books/Audio Books: Jay-Z Made in America (Michael Eric Dyson), Midnight Sun (Stephenie Meyer), Eloquent Rage (Brittney Cooper)

Drink(s): I love Simply Lemonade & Lacroix Sparkling Water

Beauty Product: Urban Decay All Nighter Setting Spray (*magical*)

Hobbies: I'm enjoying cooking Keto-friendly meals with my Ninja Foodi, crafting and designing cool things using my Cricut Explore Air 2, making beautiful intention candles (@invitaitononlycandleco) & indulging in Vin Yasa Yoga & Peloton Meditations.

Namaste

Freedom, Power, Joy, & Balance

I've often been confronted about Dream Living. I've literally had people approach me and ask how I define my dream life. My answer is always this, "Once I realized what my dream life was "not" I truly began living." The three components one must have while building their dream is *passion, purpose and power*. You know this by now. These key elements play a critical role in helping you to build a life you love. In addition to those elements, there are important fundamentals that exist while living, laughing, and walking in your dream.

Freedom: For me, freedom has come at a price of using my creativity and gifts and creating magic from them. I am living my best life when I'm able to have an idea, and turn it into a product/service (books, retreats, one-on-one sessions, digital content), or when I'm able to pursue a passion project (youth travel, committee chairing, sneakers, art, etc.). <u>*These are the things that make my life rich, and these are my dreams turned into reality.*</u> Freedom has been an amazing part of my dream life. I'll say that I vividly remember the time when I was so crippled by fear and confusion that all of the "great" stuff inside of me just sat dormant. My dreams are now free, and I exercise my freedom to live the dream life I've strategically built. I can't imagine a barrier that wouldn't allow otherwise.

Power: While power is one of my key components for dreambuilding, power is also key for dream living. Power is the tenacity and confidence it takes to *"do," "learn," and "grow."* While freedom gives me the space to create, power gives me the boldness I need to execute. *It also gives me the confidence to fail, to continually learn, and to try again.* I love that power is an internal and external strength. It has proven true to me that you will naturally feel weakened while pursuing your dream. I have had the opportunity to fail and feel totally discouraged. The moments I wanted to throw in the towel definitely have crossed my path a time or two. It is my power that connects to something bigger than me and reminds me of my infinite purpose. It's also purpose that God has granted because HE gifted me with my gifts. A word! I live my dream life because I have the power to play on my freedom. I have the power to do the things I love. I have the power to go and visit the places I dream about. I have the power to change and impact lives, daily. I have the power to live where I choose. I have the power to make new friends and connect with powerful women. I have the power to bring powerful women together. I have the power to feel really good about myself. I have the power to try new, exciting adventures. I have the power to do anything I absolutely please. Power is truly that bold confidence and expertise you possess while living your dream. I am boldly walking in my purpose and continually building a life that offers no limits. That's my dream and my power.

Joy & Balance: These two concepts go hand in hand because you absolutely have to love "all" that you've built once you begin dream living. It's definitely not as easy as it sounds or seems. Joy comes from knowing that your life is purposeful and full and rich in experiences and impact. It's a true joy when you can smile at what you're doing. Balance is when you're doing so much that you have to level it out and make sure that you're prioritizing where your joy exists. I can't spend all my time working on or in my businesses, I absolutely have to make time for my family, my friends, my job, and the other things that are important to me. In the past, I have been stuck working non-stop on my dream, and that my friend, is not joy. It's passionate chaos that quickly leads to burnout. Don't be that person. *<u>Have great joy in the life you build, but also manage your time wisely.</u>* Schedule time to be with yourself and others. I wouldn't be able to live my dream life without my Bible studies with friends, girl chats, obsessive Audible and podcast listening, fitness routines, and cooking, amongst a million other things. Many people don't know that I love cooking. I've just been blessed with a husband who cooks more often than I do, but I love trying new recipes. I have to balance time for those joyful things in my life.

As you continue to build your dream, make sure you are strategically designing a life you love. These things will empower you and keep you on a path toward success and fulfillment. As you evaluate your vision and even as it evolves, keep these elements in mind. **Make sure you give yourself permission for freedom, power, joy, and balance!**

"I have no fear in trying new things and that is my real power"
-Kiylise M. Lowe

Notes:

Chapter 2 Recap

	Chapter 2: Evaluating Plans & Goals
Visiting Your Values	Connect your values to your why.
The Formula	Connecting your Passion, Purpose, & Power.
Goals & Confidence	Setting goals that make you feel good and move boldly.
SMARTIE Goals	Create and commit to SMARTIE Goals.
Commitments	Take a look at what's on your plate.
Evaluate: Money Management	Explore where you currently spend money.
Evaluate Money Habits	Explore the things you wish you could afford.
Dream Budget	Create a budget for your dream life.
Dream Life Fund	Creating a list of things you can buy using your difference from your budget.
Investment	Learn all about investing in yourself.
Return On Investment	Assess your returns on investment.
Toolkits & Resources	Create a list of available resources.
Dream Goal Overview	List your top dream goals and desired completion dates.
Evaluation Roadmap	Reflect on your overall plan and goal.
Inspiration Station	Short Reads (Insights, Tips, etc.).
Notes	For you to create.

Chapter 3

Establish An Identity

Your Dream Identity

*H*ello Dreamer!

You are certainly on a roll! Thus far you've envisioned your vision (dream living) and you've evaluated your goals and plans to make sure they're aligned with your values. Maybe you didn't take that route and this is the first chapter you're landing on, there is no right or wrong way to build. Whatever the case may be, I extend a glorious welcome. This next area or step along the journey is all about personification. Your dream life deserves an identity. It becomes that much more attainable and tangible when you can begin branding your goal, no matter what it may be. Whether your dream is starting a family or opening a store, these activities will inform your launch plan and how you move. I want you to know that before this process was wrapped and packaged in a sequential paperback, I used these same activities and worksheets to help create my dream life. I mapped out the things I wanted, from launching this book to working on my passion projects in my community. Each time I've encountered a new goal, I've worked through these activities and exercises for clarity. *Lets Build!*

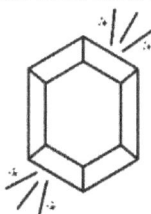

Creating Your Dream Profile

This exercise requires a bit of creativity and a lot of realness and will give you an opportunity to establish and visualize how someone living in their purpose looks, feels, sounds, and more. You can feel free to map out your current situation or where you see yourself being in the near future:

Name:
Nickname/Alias:
Birth month/Zodiac Sign:
Age/Generation:
Marital Status:
Hometown/Neighborhood:
Current Residence:
Home Structure (Apt, House, Rent, Own):
Mode of Transportation:
Career/Job/Side Hustle/Business/Dream:

The Dream Building Diary | your personal journey to creating and living the life of your dreams

Financial/Economic Status:
Education Status or Training:
Personal Goals/Passions:
Fears/Barriers:
Friend Circle/Tribe:
Personality Type/Characteristics:
Spiritual Life:
Lifestyle/Wellness:
Motivations/Inspirations/Heroes/Sheroes:

Create. Sketch. Go.

Draw | Doodle | Get Creative

Identifying Your Ideal Customer, Client, or Supporter

Now that you've visualized and established who you will be as you launch your dream, let's think about who your supporters are. This activity will help you understand who you'll need to engage in the next chapter:

Name/Nickname/Alias:
Age:
Career/Job/Hustle:
Financial Status:
Home Structure:
Marital Status/Parenthood:
Social Life:
Fears/Barriers:
Passions/Motivations/Inspirations:
Style/Lifestyle:
Wellness Lifestyle:
Social Media Platforms:
Other:
Other:

Chapter 3: Establish an Identity

Create. Sketch. Go.

Draw | Doodle | Get Creative

Dream Identity

Who are you? What sets you apart from others? Your brand identity should be unique, consistent, and reflective of your vision.

Strengths:

Growth Opportunities:

Passions:

Purpose:

Chapter 3: Establish an Identity

Project Identity

Use this page to brainstorm your project identity:

Passion Project Name | Business Name:

_____

_____

Logo (visual representation) or brand mantra (statement or slogan):

_____

_____

Website Name | Email Address Name:

_____

_____

What is the purpose of your website?

_____

_____

What functionality does your site need?

_____

_____

Chapter 3: Establish an Identity

Mood Board

The Dream Building Diary | your personal journey to creating and living the life of your dreams

Mood Board

Power 5: Words that tell your story

Example: transparent, empowering, creative, magnetic, etc.

1.

2.

3.

4.

5.

Power 5: Images that tell your story

Sketch. Doodle. Draw. Create

After establishing the mood of your dream goal, dive a little deeper, and explore the tangible pieces. What font styles interest you? What color palettes invite others? These items become staples in your brand. Use this page to brainstorm things here:

FONTS or TYPEFACE:

COLOR PALETTE: An HTML color code is an identifier used to represent a color on the web. Hexadecimal triplets represent the **colors** red, green, and blue (#RRGGBB)

Social Media

What social media platforms will you leverage? Use the space below to brainstorm social media handle names, themed content, or frequency of posting:

Platform	Handle/Page Name	[x]	Frequency
Facebook			
Instagram			
Twitter			
Snapchat			
Slack			
Blog			
YouTube			
TikTok			
Other:			

Dream Profile

Name of Business/Project:	
Logo/Mantra Statement:	
Target Client/Supporter:	
Website/Email Address:	
Social Media Handles:	
What do you offer/solve/do?	
When will this be available?	
Resources Needed:	
Accountability Partner:	

Dream Profile

Name of Business/Project:	
Logo/Mantra Statement:	
Target Client/Supporter:	
Website/Email Address:	
Social Media Handles:	
What do you offer/solve/do?	
When will this be available?	
Resources Needed:	
Accountability Partner:	

Dream Profile

Name of Business/Project:	
Logo/Mantra Statement:	
Target Client/Supporter:	
Website/Email Address:	
Social Media Handles:	
What do you offer/solve/do?	
When will this be available?	
Resources Needed:	
Accountability Partner:	

Product/Service Pricing/Time Investment

Product:
Service:
Goal:

Cost to Produce [What are your overhead costs?]:

_____

_____

Time to Produce/Execute [How much is your time worth?]:

_____

_____

Market Price [How much will you sell your product for? What will you profit?]:

_____

_____

Notes:

_____

_____

_____

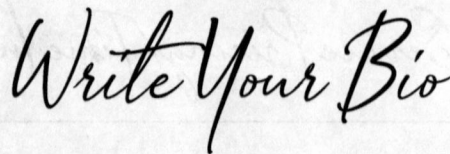

Write Your Bio

- Begin writing your bio with your first and last name.
- State your current position and what you do.
- Include at least one professional accomplishment.
- Describe your values and how they inform your career.
- Briefly tell your readers who you are outside of work.

Outline:

Biography

The Dream Building Diary | your personal journey to creating and living the life of your dreams

Chapter 3: Establish an Identity

Brand Interview

What are you currently working on?

_____

_____

What excites you about this project?

_____

_____

When people see you or your work, what do you want them to feel?

_____

_____

What do you want others to know about it?

_____

_____

Who or what has influenced you?

_____

_____

Quote Worthy

As you explore more about establishing an identity for your dream, use this page as a brainstorming dump. My favorite thing to do is to search for quotes that apply to whatever topic I'm researching. Grab your favorites about branding and drop them below:

Quote Worthy

Chapter 3: Establish an Identity

Quote Worthy

Inspirtation

Station

Establishing Your Identity Now, Rebranding Later

Great! You're doing the work. You've been establishing the identity of your dream business, passion project, event, travel, podcast, book, product, etc. You may feel like you need more time and more clarity before you get started. I'm here to tell you that you have to give exactly what you have at this moment. If you continue waiting for perfection, you'll never get your great start. If I waited until I had enough money to do certain things, I never would have been tempted to find a plethora of resources to make things work.

Launch your brand exactly as it stands today and rebrand later if needed. Some of your favorite brands have rebranded their look and overall feel time and time again. Things shift as they should, and you don't have to have everything pretty and perfectly wrapped before you can begin. *Begin, grow, glow, and do it all again.* As you personify the things you want most in your life, be sure to stay true to your values and vision. Trust me, overthinking your brand identity can lead you down a path to nowhere, or shall I say back to the drawing board. Clarity is key during this process. I hope these activities have helped you paint a visual picture, but also reinforced the key elements of dreambuilding. Connect your passion and purpose.

"The keys to brand success are self-definition, transparency, authenticity and accountability"
— Simon Mainwaring

Vending, Sponsorships, & Freebies

Vending Opportunities: If your dream includes selling a product or service then vending opportunities are a great way to establish your identity while also engaging with consumers and other business owners. Find events that fit your niche and pay to host a vendor's table (if offered). This is a great opportunity to meet people and hold a conversation about what you offer. Vending is hard work and your table presentation should look really great, but I love that you get to laser focus on your selling skills.

Sponsorships: Another great way to establish your brand identity is to become a sponsor for industry-specific events. If you're a beauty product distributor, then purchasing a sponsorship package at a beauty conference will help your product get seen by the masses. You should play in your arena. Get your brand out there so people know how to direct others to you. Think about the times you've referred someone to someone else you've never even purchased from. That's a strong identity.

Freebies: Free products, samples, calls or downloads are a must for building email lists and funneling new customers or clients to your product or service. Plan to gain interest by giving a taste of what you offer. I love giving out free digital downloads. They're typically worksheets or eBooks that I've already created. Purposely repurpose!

Notes:

Chapter 3 Recap

Chapter 3: Establishing An Identity	
Creating Your Dream Profile	Personify your dream idea.
Create. Sketch. Go	Space to sketch and doodle.
Identifying Your Ideal Person	Explore your ideal audience member.
Create. Sketch. Go.	Space to sketch and doodle.
Dream Identity	Assess who you want to be as you live your dream life.
Project Identity Planning	Explore the specifications of your next project (needs).
Mood Board	Create the vibe you want others to feel.
Power 5	Describe your brand in 5 words & images.
Style Guide	Create a style guide filled with brand identifiers.
Social Media Leverage	Discover how you will utilize social media to establish an identity.
Dream Profile	Drill down on characteristics of your dream goal.
Investment	Identify the value or worth of your dream goal.
Write Your Bio	Write your biography.
Brand Interview	Assess your dream brand.
Quote Worthy	Explore your favorite inspirational quotes.
Inspiration Station	Short Reads (Insights, Tips, etc.)
Notes	For you to create.

Chapter 4

Engage Others

Engage Others

Let's talk about community for a moment. The power of the community you build and the way you impact others matter. These things matter even when you can't see how. I remember being super secretive about things I worked on because of fear of jinxing myself or being vulnerable to negative thoughts. I wanted to protect those things that were dear to me. That's not at all what dream living is about. It is, of course, for your own desire and God's glory, but you will also inevitably inherit the role of "light shiner." As you unapologetically live a life you love, your inner light will radiate outwardly. Once you step into this new role, you'll need to have a strategy to engage others. My strategy was based on the things I didn't find in my research. I was bombarded by these powerhouse, boss women entrepreneurs all over social media and oftentimes I felt that they were super talented, gifted, or lucky because things just seemed so perfect. In actuality, I knew that life had lots of peaks and valleys for those women. They weren't exempt, no one is. I was just desiring to hear how they stumbled and overcame their setbacks. I needed that narrative.

It was my decision to engage with other dreamers by simply revealing that narrative. I shared my failures, my pain points, and my challenges. I wanted to be completely transparent in hopes of showing that success looks great and feels great, but challenges are the true learning blocks of life and they hurt like hell. Ouch! They're discouraging and sometimes super overwhelming, and oftentimes you're only as great as the team behind you that keeps you going. I've endured times of transition and pivots and the confirmation to keep me going came from a fellow dreamer who would randomly reach out to me. There were many times when I've felt so connected to dreamers on their journey while battling if mine was worth it. I'm just being honest here. It was the engagement that helped me.

*I*n this chapter, you will explore ways to engage others. You'll begin by assessing the community you've already built and thinking of the community you need to recruit. You'll create a plan of action that'll help you become visible. This may be scary for some, as you desire to not share outwardly, but I promise, there is so much power in revealing your truth (#freedom). One of my favorite quotes is, *"You have to release for increase."* Let's build teams, share our dreams, and engage others in the process.

> *"The power to build community is the power for others to see you and what you bring to the table."*
>
> —Kiylise Lowe

Dream Teams & Things

When building your mountainous dream life that infuses your passion, power, and purpose, it is only right to know the key players in your corner. To assemble or assess your Dream Team, you're going to need a good balance of the right folk.

The Encourager: This person keeps you motivated and encouraged. It may be by affirming words or modeled behavior, but there will be times when the life you want to live in your dreams are not matching up to your reality. You need an encourager on your team.

The Idea Bouncer: This person understands what a necessary brainstorming session looks like. You're going to need someone to run by some of your craziest, but most genius, out-of-this-world dreams, and ideas.

The Straight-No Chaser: This person will unapologetically shut you down (all in love). You might experience hurt feelings or moments of discourse, but this person is simply going to tell you their truth. It's great to make sure you're not surrounded by a bunch of *Yes* peeps.

The Logical One: This person is the Ying to your Yang. They will think of everything you won't. They'll play Devil's Advocate during decision-making and keep you abreast of various perspectives. It's great to have someone with a mind as such.

The Hand Holder: This person is always rooting for you. Right, wrong, or in between, they'll have your back 100 percent. They'll hold your hand and ride this wave with you. There may be moments when they can't see any of your faults or flaws, but ultimately you can count on this person to believe in you as you build.

The Dreamer: This person lives their own dream life. They sometimes march to the beat of their own drum, but they completely understand the journey you're on. They've been there before. They've mastered connecting their passion, purpose, and power, and they're continually inspiring you. This is a dynamic team player for your roster.

Ultimately, a great mix of all of these personality types will help build your DREAM TEAM.

Where do you see yourself within these categories?

Where do your friends see you within these categories?

Dream Teams Goals (AF)

Now that I've given you a starting lineup to help inform your dreambuilding process, let's look at how I've grouped some of my own squad. Soon, you'll name or create a plan for the people you need on your team. Stay tuned.

Your Bests/Lifelines - These are your very best friends. The people you couldn't imagine life without - your **true soulmates**. They love the ugly parts of you, yet still admire your beauty. They won't bite their tongue when you're wrong or selfish or being difficult. Your lifelines inspire you to do better, to be better, yet always make you feel better. They're the most important and consistent people on your dream team. They are literally your **everything**.

Your Squad - Yesss! Your squad is diverse altogether. Your squad consists of a group of people who come together in genuine love. You can chill together, share intellectual conversations, party, travel, grieve, and more. Nothing is off-limits when you're together. It's your squad that you ride with and have the best fun with. **Unforgettable memories**. It's a party anytime my squad (The Team) comes together. Our random fun is most invigorating. <u>*I love the diversity and complexity of my squad.*</u> We're so different yet work so well.

Your Pro's - Sometimes in life you just have different folks for different strokes. As different as your professional life may be from your squad or your bests, you absolutely need your pro's (or tribe). Pro's are designated individuals who share similar **professional goals** with you. Your pro's are always down to network, come up with new ideas, talk business, and ultimately make more money, and do lots of good in the world. These are the people who you connect with on that level. You can call your pro's when you find a cool event on Eventbrite or stumble upon an upcoming conference. You can call your pro's when you're ready to leave your job and step into something greater. Your pro's know all about working and grinding, and they share valuable experiences. Your pro's may even be your mentors. The one who has been some places. <u>**My pro's are so bomb.**</u> They keep me grounded in the work I do, but also inspire me to do more. They are also a super blast to be around. (*Hey Soul Tribe.*)

Your Babes- Babes are those you just magically connect with. It can be that one coworker you really gel with or even your hairstylist. Babes not only respect your point of view but they're also easy to talk to. They give you **good advice** and don't mind telling their opinion. They're people you can agree to disagree with. How lovely! You might not hang out all the time, but you know a time to do so is always on the table. <u>**Babes are fun,**</u> and although there might not be a said long-term investment, there will be short-term gratification that makes your heart warm right when you need it. These are the relationships that make sense without you even realizing.

Chapter 4: Engage Others

Add your own Dream Team categories:

Dream Team Goals

Take a moment to write who's currently on your Dream Team. List their name and what role they play within your life. You may also take this time to list what role you serve in their lives as well. Begin with your top 5:

TOP 5	

Net Worth, Net Work

Your dream life is only as strong as the people you choose to have in your circle. It's time to begin drafting the people who have influence in your life. It may be an old friend, teacher, mentor, or coach. They should be able to provide something to your NET WORTH. Jot down names, numbers, addresses, social media handles, etc. Focus on your Top 10:

Social Media Engagement

What are your social media profiles?

_____

_____

How does your audience vary on each platform?

_____

_____

Do you currently engage with others by way of comments, questions, polls, etc.?

_____

_____

_____

In what ways can you use social media to engage with others and gain potential supporters?

_____

_____

_____

_____

Engaging Others by Feedback

Research is a critical practice in dream living. We pretty much conduct research each and every day as we browse the Internet and social media platforms. Another way to engage others is to gather feedback and opinions. Grow a following by allowing others to be heard on your platform. Think of how you engage with people online. In what ways do you find yourself connected to someone's content?

Brainstorm ways you can engage others:

Features & Content Series

Features: Content that highlight another person for a particular purpose- allows another person to market your offering to their audience (casting the net).

Series: More than one offering of content that typically scaffolds consecutively- a series gives followers something to look forward to (continual engagement).

Brainstorm Ways You Can Create Content that includes Features:

Brainstorm Ways You Can Create Content in Series form:

Collaborations

Collaborations: Opportunities for shared engagement- to collaborate with another person on a particular project sharing different opinions and perspectives.

As you build your dream life, list some ways you can collaborate with others (podcasts, blog features, vlogs, panel discussions, etc.) and who you'd be interested in working with.

1.

2.

3.

4.

5.

6.

7.

8.

9.

10.

Engagement by Pitching

Pitch: A presentation of your dream idea to someone with the ability to invest a resource or to sell your offering.

Pitching is an acquired skill. The more you do it, the better you become. I've had the opportunity to pitch some ideas a few times and I will say that you have to know your stuff inside and out. If you're a fan of the hit TV show *Shark Tank,* just as much as I am then you've seen how the financial discussion is usually what turns a shark's eye. While I pray *Shark Tank* is in your near future, I want you to start preparing with basic steps toward pitching. You can never be too prepared.

Steps for creating a solid pitch:

1. Tell your Story: Why are you focused on your idea?
2. Provide a sample or give a demonstration.
3. Solve my problem: What makes me a hero after being engaged in your product or service. How will it change my life?
4. Know your worth: Know your financials---which means "pilots and prototypes" are a thing. The best advice I could give is to start where you are, begin with what you have, and tweak later. You should test your idea before pitching.
5. Rinse and Repeat.

Pitching Practice

Open with a statement or question (your hook):

Tell who you are. Describe yourself and your dream idea:

Tell what problem you solve with your idea:

Describe how your idea is different from others and the advantage someone would gain by working with you:

All About Freebies

What is a freebie?

A freebie is content or products you offer complimentary to help establish your identity, build rapport, and build relationships. A freebie spotlights your values, mission, and commitment to your goal (if you're an awesome writer, your free content will shine light on your awesomeness). It also helps solve a problem or shed light on a problem you're solving in your life (lessons learned).

Types of Freebies (also called Opt-Ins):

[ ] eBooks & Workbooks
[ ] Infographics
[ ] Resource Lists
[ ] Fillable PDF's
[ ] Video Tutorials
[ ] Discovery Calls
[ ] Webinars

Step 1: What's in it for someone?
Step 2: Outline how you present or package the problem you're solving or answering?
Step 3: What do you need to collect email information to begin building your list? How will you facilitate sign ups?
Step 4: Create your freebie & offer (discount or promo).

Freebie Creation Ideas

Frequently Asked Questions (about something you offer; maybe you've self-published a book and you want to give an FAQ sheet).

Process or Workflow (how do you allow systems to work for you?):

Blog Posts or Articles (tips, steps, or tricks to help solve a problem):

Resource Guides (tools and websites that can help others):

What can you create that provides:

> A spotlight on your mission and values & essentially on your commitment to your dream idea

&

> An actionable value to someone that ultimately helps solve a problem or pain point

Quick Write Moment

When you think of engaging others in your dream idea, business, product, service, or goal, what type of engagement makes sense for you? What feels uncomfortable about engagement and how can you overcome it? Use the next few pages to reflect. Outline below:

_____
_____
_____
_____
_____
_____
_____
_____
_____
_____
_____
_____
_____
_____

Inspirtation Station

Engaging by Documenting

*H*ey Dreamers,

As you engage clients, customers, or just supporters with your dream, you've got to get comfortable with documenting. Grab your camera and snap pics to record the magical moments in your life. Dream living comes with a special charge. It's like each one, teach one. You have to share your journey so that others know of the possibilities.

If you're a writer, begin writing. If you're interested in owning a brick-and-mortar business start now with an online entity. Get visible, get your name out there. Garner the support of others while inspiring change agents at the same time. This is the requirement of dream living that people often forget to explain. Once you get, you have to give.

Ways you can become visible:

- Start a Blog.
- Utilize social media Lives.
- Join FB groups & network.
- Email potential mentors.
- Volunteer, volunteer, volunteer.

Dining with Dreams

*D*ining with Dreams is an amazing storytelling platform that invites phenomenal women to be featured as keynote speakers or workshop facilitators during a breakfast, brunch, lunch, or dinner experience. I created this event after realizing the valuable wealth of knowledge that many women had to share. These women may never get an opportunity to share their stories in an intimate setting that changes the lives of others. The women who become audience members may never encounter these particular stories in this setting. I wanted to provide them with intimacy, psychological safety, and unwavering support during this event. A space to share their very own tea and triumph testimonies.

I engaged with a handful of women who specifically reached out to me after the conclusion of my first Dream Retreat. Once the Dream Retreat concluded, I posted our incredible experience on my blog, social media platforms, and e-newsletter. I shared what others had missed. When I encourage you to share about the things you do it's because sometimes people are unaware of their own pain points and the things they're missing. **Engage** with them in that way and make some of your own dreams come to life. This is exactly what I did and now Dining with Dreams is one of my signature events.

Tips to Empower Your Team

HONESTY - the good, the bad, the ugly! Honesty is major 🔑🔑🔑🔑. You have to have brutally honest relationships with your team to be able to tell them when they're wrong. They appreciate your candidness. It's critical for empowering your team for greatness. Sometimes my friends don't even have to speak, and I know exactly what they're thinking, so I check myself...that's empowering!

AFFIRMATIONS - Affirming your team and reminding them that they're super lit is powerful! You have to <u>pour into the people around you.</u> It is far too often that we lack daily self-affirmation and support. Take a moment to send a text about how great of a parent or student your friend may be. Take a second to compliment how beautiful or fine they look. It's up to us to continually build up and affirm the people we love.

INCLUSION - *Share your world* – Include your team into your gifts and passions even if they don't share those same values. It's polite to extend an invitation or share what's going on in your world. We sometimes leave out the people who love us most because of their own interests. It's empowering to know what your closet friends have going on. I brag about my team all the time because I'm so enamored by the things they're doing in their lives.

ADVICE - Ask, ask, and ask - When in doubt, ask your team, WWYD (what would you do?). These are the people who won't hold you up and although you may agree to disagree, it's empowering to know that you care enough to ask. I love to ask my friends for daily weather advice...like every morning I'm shooting a text to my bestie that reads "Is it ok to wear sandals yet?" 😂😂😂😂 I can count on her to not have me out here looking bold and cold. Just ask.

CONSISTENCY - The final tip for empowering your team is **keeping it consistent**. Keep tips 1-4 up and repeat over and over again. You share life with these people, so you have to continue being honest, affirming, inclusive, and seeking advice. These are the things that keep the wheels turning and blood pumping. It's about the relationships you build. Your team will appreciate you and feel empowered to keep dreaming and teaming with you.

Empower.

Notes:

Chapter 4 Recap

	Chapter 4: Engage Others
Dream Teams & Things	Explore the characteristics of players needed for your team.
Dream Teams Goals	Explore the balance of characteristics needed for your dream team.
Net Worth, Net Work	Assess who you already have in your circle.
Social Media Engagement	Evaluate how you engage using social media.
Engaging Others by Feedback	Create opportunities to gather feedback.
Features & Content Series	Understand how to make features and series work for you.
Collaborations	Identify an array of collaboration opportunities.
Engagement by Pitching	Gain exposure through the art of pitching.
Pitching Practice	Draft an outline of a pitch.
All About Freebies	Explore how freebies help with gaining followership.
Freebie Creation Ideas	A list of freebies you can create.
Quick Write	Brainstorm how to engage others in your dream process.
Inspiration Station	Short Reads (Insights, Tips, etc.)
Notes	For you to create.

Execute The Dream

Experience The Outcomes

Chapter 5

Execute the Dream

Experience the Outcomes

*H*ello Dreamer!

I can't believe we're already in Chapter 5. I'm so excited for you and the work you've done. This workbook/journal/diary was created with you in mind. Don't ever forget I was once "*you*," seeking a place to organize my thoughts and do more self-discovery.

*Y*ou have now walked through <u>Envisioning Your Vision</u> by big picture conceptualizing. With your vision a little clearer, you've <u>Evaluated Your Plans and Goals</u> and the approach you're going to take to build your dream. You've learned how to <u>Establish An Identity</u> for your dream idea to visually bring it to life. You've also dabbled with how to <u>Engage Others</u> to support your dream idea. You've walked through steps and tips that will help you share your story and now you've arrived at the most important step of them all. Welcome to Chapter 5. It's time to <u>Execute Your Dream and Experience the Outcomes</u>. You have an amazing outline and in this chapter, you are going to create launch plans and task lists. It's blueprint time. There's going to be lots of repetitive space to figure out all the fine details and to plan and reflect. You'll see multiple working pages to hold the multiple dreams you may have. *Lets Launch!*

If you're like, "OK, I have a pretty clear vision of what I want to do." Now, this is when I charge and challenge you to continue on with the journey. Flow & Go!

Brainstorm
(organize your thoughts)

Plan
(daily, monthly, quarterly, yearly, big picture)

Design
(curate a visual)

Prototype
(produce your dream & your purpose)

Launch
(take the stage)

Iterate
(reflect & tweak your passion)

Experience it Again
(execute & live in your power)

Dream Brainstorm

Idea

Chapter 5: Execute the Dream | Experience the Outcomes

Dream Brainstorm

Dream Brainstorm

Chapter 5: Execute the Dream | Experience the Outcomes

Dream Brainstorm

Dream Brainstorm

Idea

Project Identity Brainstorm

Use this page to brainstorm your project identity

Passion Project Name| Business Name:

_____

Logo (visual representation) or brand mantra (statement or slogan):

_____

Website Name | Email Address Name:

_____

What is the purpose of your website?

_____

_____

What functionality does your site need? (Scheduler, payment processing, mailing list forms, etc.)

_____

_____

_____

The Dream Building Diary | your personal journey to creating and living the life of your dreams

Project Identity Brainstorm

Use this page to brainstorm your project identity

Passion Project Name| Business Name:

_____

Logo (visual representation) or brand mantra (statement or slogan):

_____

Website Name | Email Address Name:

_____

What is the purpose of your website?

_____

_____

What functionality does your site need? (Scheduler, payment processing, mailing list forms, etc.)

_____

_____

_____

Project Identity Brainstorm

Use this page to brainstorm your project identity

Passion Project Name| Business Name:

_____

Logo (visual representation) or brand mantra (statement or slogan):

_____

Website Name | Email Address Name:

_____

What is the purpose of your website?

_____

_____

What functionality does your site need? (Scheduler, payment processing, mailing list forms, etc.)

_____

_____

_____

The Dream Building Diary | your personal journey to creating and living the life of your dreams

Project Identity Brainstorm

Use this page to brainstorm your project identity

Passion Project Name| Business Name:

___

Logo (visual representation) or brand mantra (statement or slogan):

___

Website Name | Email Address Name:

___

What is the purpose of your website?

___

___

What functionality does your site need? (Scheduler, payment processing, mailing list forms, etc.)

___

___

___

Chapter 5: Execute the Dream | Experience the Outcomes

Project Identity Brainstorm

Use this page to brainstorm your project identity

Passion Project Name| Business Name:

_____

Logo (visual representation) or brand mantra (statement or slogan):

_____

Website Name | Email Address Name:

_____

What is the purpose of your website?

_____

_____

What functionality does your site need? (Scheduler, payment processing, mailing list forms, etc.)

_____

_____

_____

The Dream Building Diary | your personal journey to creating and living the life of your dreams

Build & Balance Action Sheets

Date:_____   *Today's Big Three Goals*

[ ]	
[ ]	
[ ]	

Task Break Down & To-Do's

Big Picture Goals

Build & Balance Action Sheets

Date:_____   *Today's Big Three Goals*

[ ]	
[ ]	
[ ]	

Task Break Down & To-Do's

Big Picture Goals

The Dream Building Diary | your personal journey to creating and living the life of your dreams

Build & Balance Action Sheets

Date:_____ *Today's Big Three Goals*

[ ]	
[ ]	
[ ]	

Task Break Down & To-Do's

Big Picture Goals

Chapter 5: Execute the Dream | Experience the Outcomes

Build & Balance Action Sheets

Date:_____ *Today's Big Three Goals*

[ ]	
[ ]	
[ ]	

Task Break Down & To-Do's

Big Picture Goals

The Dream Building Diary | your personal journey to creating and living the life of your dreams

Build & Balance Action Sheets

Date:_____   *Today's Big Three Goals*

[ ]	
[ ]	
[ ]	

Task Break Down & To-Do's

Big Picture Goals

Chapter 5: Execute the Dream | Experience the Outcomes

Monthly Plan & Prep

My Mantra this Month:

Inspiration (books, bloggers, podcasts, shows):

Self-Care (what do I need to do for me):

Big Picture Goals:

# Monthly Plan & Prep

My Mantra this Month:

Inspiration (books, bloggers, podcasts, shows):

Self-Care (what do I need to do for me):

Big Picture Goals:

Monthly Plan & Prep

My Mantra this Month:

Inspiration (books, bloggers, podcasts, shows):

Self-Care (what do I need to do for me):

Big Picture Goals:

Monthly Plan & Prep

My Mantra this Month:

Inspiration (books, bloggers, podcasts, shows):

Self-Care (what do I need to do for me):

Big Picture Goals:

Chapter 5: Execute the Dream | Experience the Outcomes

Monthly Plan & Prep

My Mantra this Month:

Inspiration (books, bloggers, podcasts, shows):

Self-Care (what do I need to do for me):

Big Picture Goals:

30, 60, 90 Day Goal Setting

January	February

March	I will complete:

30, 60, 90 Day Goal Setting

April	May

June	I will complete:

30, 60, 90 Day Goal Setting

July	August

September:	I will complete:

30, 60, 90 Day Goal Setting

October	November

December	I will complete:

30, 60, 90 Day Goal Setting

Quarterly Planning

Q1: January-March

Q2: April-June

Q3: July-September

Q4: October-December

Notes:

Quarterly Planning

Q1: January-March

Q2: April-June

Q3: July-September

Q4: October-December

Notes:

Chapter 5: Execute the Dream | Experience the Outcomes

Quarterly Planning

Q1: January-March

Q2: April-June

Q3: July-September

Q4: October-December

Notes:

Quarterly Planning

Q1: January-March

Q2: April-June

Q3: July-September

Q4: October-December

Notes:

Chapter 5: Execute the Dream | Experience the Outcomes

Quarterly Planning

Q1: January-March
Q2: April-June
Q3: July-September
Q4: October-December

Notes:

Yearly Planning

January	
February	
March	
April	
May	
June	

Yearly Planning

July	
August	
September	
October	
November	
December	

Yearly Planning

January	
February	
March	
April	
May	
June	

Yearly Planning

July	
August	
September	
October	
November	
December	

Yearly Big Picture Planning

Design Blueprint

Design the vision for your dream goal (product, service, event, lifestyle change, etc.). Use these pages for to creatively sketch, doodle, or draw.

Design Blueprint

Sketch. Doodle. Draw.

Chapter 5: Execute the Dream | Experience the Outcomes

Design Blueprint
Sketch. Doodle. Draw.

Design Blueprint

Sketch. Doodle. Draw.

Design Blueprint

Describe the vision for your dream goal (product, service, event, lifestyle change, etc.).

_____

_____

_____

_____

_____

_____

_____

_____

_____

_____

_____

_____

_____

_____

_____

This is a Launch Plan Outline

Envision The Vision: What is your idea and what problem does it solve or accomplish in your life or the lives of others?

> *Write your vision here. Include your mission statement, power words, and values in this section.*

Evaluate Plans & Goals: How will you make your idea a reality and what tasks do you need to complete to make sure it happens?

> *Think about the major tasks you need to complete to achieve your goal, like creating content, hiring outside help, purchasing supplies, etc. Include a few action steps you'll take and the people you'll need to contact.*

Establish An Identity: What's your brand identity for this idea and what mood or feeling does it project?

> *Talk about your ideal brand identity and the feeling you want to project to others. Think about brands that resonate with you. Share your reasoning and approach here.*

Engage Others: Who is your audience and what measures will you take to gain their trust or support of your idea?

> *Describe who your audience is (women, men, youth, millennials, etc.) and talk about the ways you plan to connect with them (social media, events, etc.).*

Execute The Dream | Experience the Outcomes: What date will you go live with prototyping/field testing your idea?

> *Write your proposed launch date here (be specific & include a time) and also share how you plan to document your progress (surveys, video footage, pictures, testimonials, etc.).*

Launch Plan Outline

Envision The Vision: What is your idea and what problem does it solve or accomplish in your life or the lives of others?

_____

_____

Evaluate Plans & Goals: How will you make your idea a reality and what tasks do you need to complete to make sure it happens?

_____

_____

Establish An Identity: What's your brand identity for this idea and what mood or feeling does it project?

_____

_____

Engage Others: Who is your audience and what measures will you take to gain their trust or support of your idea?

_____

_____

Execute The Dream | Experience the Outcomes: What date will you go live with prototyping/field testing your idea and how will you document it?

_____

Launch Plan Outline

Envision The Vision: What is your idea and what problem does it solve or accomplish in your life or the lives of others?

_____

_____

Evaluate Plans & Goals: How will you make your idea a reality and what tasks do you need to complete to make sure it happens?

_____

_____

Establish An Identity: What's your brand identity for this idea and what mood or feeling does it project?

_____

_____

Engage Others: Who is your audience and what measures will you take to gain their trust or support of your idea?

_____

_____

Execute The Dream | Experience the Outcomes: What date will you go live with prototyping/field testing your idea and how will you document it?

_____

Launch Plan Outline

Envision The Vision: What is your idea and what problem does it solve or accomplish in your life or the lives of others?

_____

_____

Evaluate Plans & Goals: How will you make your idea a reality and what tasks do you need to complete to make sure it happens?

_____

_____

Establish An Identity: What's your brand identity for this idea and what mood or feeling does it project?

_____

_____

Engage Others: Who is your audience and what measures will you take to gain their trust or support of your idea?

_____

_____

Execute The Dream | Experience the Outcomes: What date will you go live with prototyping/field testing your idea and how will you document it?

_____

Launch Plan Outline

Envision The Vision: What is your idea and what problem does it solve or accomplish in your life or the lives of others?

_____

_____

Evaluate Plans & Goals: How will you make your idea a reality and what tasks do you need to complete to make sure it happens?

_____

_____

Establish An Identity: What's your brand identity for this idea and what mood or feeling does it project?

_____

_____

Engage Others: Who is your audience and what measures will you take to gain their trust or support of your idea?

_____

_____

Execute The Dream | Experience the Outcomes: What date will you go live with prototyping/field testing your idea and how will you document it?

_____

Launch Plan Planning

Vision:

Identity:

Plans & Goals:

Engagement:

Execution:

Chapter 5: Execute the Dream | Experience the Outcomes

Launch Plan Planning

Vision:	Plans & Goals:
Identity:	**Engagement:**
	Execution:

The Dream Building Diary | your personal journey to creating and living the life of your dreams

Launch Plan Planning

Vision:

Identity:

Plans & Goals:

Engagement:

Execution:

Launch Plan Planning

Vision:

Identity:

Plans & Goals:

Engagement:

Execution:

Launch Checklist Example

Idea Name/Title:	Dining with Dreams Brunch
Date & Time:	November 17th, 2017 | 12pm-3pm
Location/URL:	The Bird & The Bread, Birmingham, MI
Task Checklist:	[✔] Secure the venue [✔] Confirm Speakers [✔] Create Flyer & [✔] Open Ticket Sales [✔] Promote on Socials/Email [✔] Choose décor & gifts [✔] Check in with venue [✔] Check in w/speakers [✔] Hire photographer [✔] Schedule walk through [✔] Update social posts [✔] Set up event [✔] Day of event execution
Accountability Partner:	JeTeia B. (Business Bestie)
Engagement Schedule:	October 12, 2017 Social posting 11am, email blast, printed flyers
Notes:	*Pick up flowers from florist on 11/17, order gift bags from Amazon by 11/15*

Chapter 5: Execute the Dream | Experience the Outcomes

Launch Plan Checklist

Idea Name/Title:	
Date & Time:	
Location/URL:	
Task Checklist:	[ ] [ ] [ ] [ ] [ ] [ ] [ ] [ ] [ ] [ ]
Accountability Partner(s):	
Engagement Schedule:	
Notes:	

The DreamBuilding Diary | your personal journey to creating and living the life of your dreams

Launch Plan Checklist

Idea Name/Title:	
Date & Time:	
Location/URL:	
Task Checklist:	[ ] [ ] [ ] [ ] [ ] [ ] [ ] [ ] [ ] [ ]
Accountability Partner(s):	
Engagement Schedule:	
Notes:	

Launch Plan Checklist

Idea Name/Title:	
Date & Time:	
Location/URL:	
Task Checklist:	[ ] [ ] [ ] [ ] [ ] [ ] [ ] [ ] [ ] [ ]
Accountability Partner(s):	
Engagement Schedule:	
Notes:	

The Dream Building Diary | your personal journey to creating and living the life of your dreams

Launch Plan Checklist

Idea Name/Title:	
Date & Time:	
Location/URL:	
Task Checklist:	[ ] [ ] [ ] [ ] [ ] [ ] [ ] [ ] [ ] [ ]
Accountability Partner(s):	
Engagement Schedule:	
Notes:	

Chapter 5: Execute the Dream | Experience the Outcomes

Monthly Reflection

Month: _____

Wins for the Month:

Growth Opportunities:

Barriers/Challenges:

Feelings Chart: Circle or doodle your emotion for this month.

Monthly Reflection

Month: _____

Wins for the Month:

Growth Opportunities:

Barriers/Challenges:

Feelings Chart: Circle or doodle your emotion for this month.

Chapter 5: Execute the Dream | Experience the Outcomes

Monthly Reflection

Month: _____

Wins for the Month:

Growth Opportunities:

Barriers/Challenges:

Feelings Chart: Circle or doodle your emotion for this month.

The DreamBuilding Diary | your personal journey to creating and living the life of your dreams

Monthly Reflection

Month: _____

Wins for the Month:

Growth Opportunities:

Barriers/Challenges:

Feelings Chart: Circle or doodle your emotion for this month.

Chapter 5: Execute the Dream | Experience the Outcomes

Monthly Reflection

Month: _____

Wins for the Month:

Growth Opportunities:

Barriers/Challenges:

Feelings Chart: Circle or doodle your emotion for this month.

The Dream Building Diary | your personal journey to creating and living the life of your dreams

Monthly Reflection

Month: _____

Wins for the Month:

Growth Opportunities:

Barriers/Challenges:

Feelings Chart: Circle or doodle your emotion for this month.

Chapter 5: Execute the Dream | Experience the Outcomes

Monthly Reflection

Month: _____

Wins for the Month:

Growth Opportunities:

Barriers/Challenges:

Feelings Chart: Circle or doodle your emotion for this month.

The Dream Building Diary | your personal journey to creating and living the life of your dreams

Monthly Reflection

Month: _____

Wins for the Month:

Growth Opportunities:

Barriers/Challenges:

Feelings Chart: Circle or doodle your emotion for this month.

Chapter 5: Execute the Dream | Experience the Outcomes

Monthly Reflection

Month: _____

Wins for the Month:

Growth Opportunities:

Barriers/Challenges:

Feelings Chart: Circle or doodle your emotion for this month.

The Dream Building Diary | your personal journey to creating and living the life of your dreams

Monthly Reflection

Month: _____

Wins for the Month:

Growth Opportunities:

Barriers/Challenges:

Feelings Chart: Circle or doodle your emotion for this month.

"People just don't understand how obsessed I am with winning"

−Kobe Bryant

Win Journal

As you execute and experience your dream, be sure to take intentional time to reflect on your wins. Even the smallest win is still a win.

List your most recent wins? What emotions are you experiencing?

_____

_____

_____

What are some growth opportunities for you? What have you learned?

_____

_____

_____

What are your next steps? How will you prepare?

_____

_____

_____

_____

Win Journal

Describe a play-by-play of how you executed your dream:

_____
_____
_____
_____
_____
_____
_____
_____
_____
_____
_____
_____
_____
_____
_____
_____
_____
_____

The Dream Building Diary | your personal journey to creating and living the life of your dreams

Win Journal

As you execute and experience your dream, be sure to take intentional time to reflect on your wins. Even the smallest win is still a win.

List your most recent wins? What emotions are you experiencing?

_____

_____

_____

What are some growth opportunities for you? What have you learned?

_____

_____

_____

What are your next steps? How will you prepare?

_____

_____

_____

_____

_____

Win Journal

Describe a play-by-play of how you executed your dream:

Win Journal

As you execute and experience your dream, be sure to take intentional time to reflect on your wins. Even the smallest win is still a win.

List your most recent wins? What emotions are you experiencing?

_____

_____

_____

What are some growth opportunities for you? What have you learned?

_____

_____

_____

What are your next steps? How will you prepare?

_____

_____

_____

_____

Chapter 5: Execute the Dream | Experience the Outcomes

Win Journal

Describe a play-by-play of how you executed your dream:

_____
_____
_____
_____
_____
_____
_____
_____
_____
_____
_____
_____
_____
_____
_____
_____
_____

Win Journal

As you execute and experience your dream, be sure to take intentional time to reflect on your wins. Even the smallest win is still a win.

List your most recent wins? What emotions are you experiencing?

_____

_____

_____

What are some growth opportunities for you? What have you learned?

_____

_____

_____

What are your next steps? How will you prepare?

_____

_____

_____

_____

Win Journal

Describe a play-by-play of how you executed your dream:

Chapter 5: Execute the Dream | Experience the Outcomes

Win Journal

As you execute and experience your dream, be sure to take intentional time to reflect on your wins. Even the smallest win is still a win.

List your most recent wins? What emotions are you experiencing?

_____

_____

_____

What are some growth opportunities for you? What have you learned?

_____

_____

_____

What are your next steps? How will you prepare?

_____

_____

_____

_____

Chapter 5: Execute the Dream | Experience the Outcomes

Win Journal

Describe a play-by-play of how you executed your dream:

Dream Tweaks

Use this space to brainstorm ways to tweak your dream idea or goal. What things can you do differently? What supports can you tap into to help you achieve your dream? What can you do to support your emotional state during the iteration phase? Think of a variety of things that will help you to continuously improve your outcomes. Use this cycle on repeat and continue dreambuilding!

Dream Tweaks

Use this space to brainstorm ways to tweak your dream idea or goal. What things can you do differently? What supports can you tap into to help you achieve your dream? What can you do to support your emotional state during the iteration phase? Think of a variety of things that will help you to continuously improve your outcomes. Use this cycle on repeat and continue dreambuilding!

Dream Tweaks

Use this space to brainstorm ways to tweak your dream idea or goal. What things can you do differently? What supports can you tap into to help you achieve your dream? What can you do to support your emotional state during the iteration phase? Think of a variety of things that will help you to continuously improve your outcomes. Use this cycle on repeat and continue dreambuilding!

Dream Tweaks

Use this space to brainstorm ways to tweak your dream idea or goal. What things can you do differently? What supports can you tap into to help you achieve your dream? What can you do to support your emotional state during the iteration phase? Think of a variety of things that will help you to continuously improve your outcomes. Use this cycle on repeat and continue dreambuilding!

Inspirtation Station

On Task, On Target

*H*ey Dreamers,

I have to admit that I am still working to master this time management thing. If you know me in "real" life then you know, I am always, always BUSY. I really want to master moving like clockwork and slaying all my goals and to-dos. Here are 4 ways that I stay on task and on target through all of it.

Tools are a gift that allow a glorious flow in your productivity. To effectively manage my time I use the iCal/Google Calendar. I love that you can keep up with your various calendars on one platform. If it's not on my calendar, it probably didn't or doesn't exist. This works really well for any backtracking you may have as well. While the app works wonders, it's my dry erase board calendar and physical planners that carry the majority of the weight. I'm a visual person, and I always need to see the big picture.

Automation is really a mindset shift. Apps such as Later and Planoly are heaven-sent. I schedule content to post to social media ahead of time. Many website platforms allow you to schedule content as well. How awesome is it for me to be at a dentist appointment while my latest blog post is going live? These things give me so much flexibility and help me to stay consistent and save time. They also keep me sane.

Timers & Alerts work miracles when trying to manage time. If I plan to work on my business, then I'll set a timer that indicates how long I have to solely focus on that. Once the timer goes off, down goes the laptop or pen, and away goes all of my DreamBuilding Co. tasks. I've started doing the same with social media, online shopping, work tasks, etc. This helps me to be accountable to myself and to manage my time wisely. I am able to focus on the most important tasks instead of being all over the place browsing IG and working on content. If you haven't done this, I encourage you to do so. As I completed the first edition of this book (The DreamBuilding Diary), I faced a hump that I just couldn't seem to get over. It wasn't until I decided that I would wake up at 5am for a week straight and spend 45 mins working on the book. This was extremely hard for me, but I got it done. Spend some time blocking off time to do certain things. There is actually enough time in the day if it's allocated properly.

Accountability is a game-changer. I frequently talk about having someone who is on your head about your goals like an accountability partner. What has really helped me manage my time and stay accountable to my goals is putting "something" out into the universe. The moment I announced my launch date for my Because Dreams Win blog, I had no choice but to complete my first round of posts, interviews, and graphics. I had spoken it into the universe and was now tasked with a deadline. The universe was holding me accountable and helping me to stay on task with managing my time. I'm also a Virgo and I heard we are perfectionists, so failure was not an option.

Balance work and play. Balance is a true test of your passion and purpose aligning. Balance is found within your power. When I wake up in the morning and go over my calendar for the day, preparing myself for whatever tasks I have, I try to make sure that there is at minimum something self-indulging on my calendar. It's usually heading to the gym in the evenings or watching a fave TV show before bed with hubs. This sounds so simple, and maybe not the grandest act of self-indulgence, but there was a time when I would go to work and come home and do more work. I was one of those people who believed "sleep is for losers" or "you can sleep when you're dead." I promise I threw those theories out of the window a long time ago. You will die if you aren't kind to your body, and rest is the key to productivity. To make sure my life is balanced I take rest seriously, and I take time to play even more seriously. I have no problem doing things that make me happy and exploring this universe with my loved ones. I enjoy laughter and great vibes so my play is very intentional and strategic. I try and celebrate everything in my life, so when I work extremely hard (as I always do), I feel so relieved to play extremely hard and celebrate this dream life I'm living. Balance is key.

While my time management tips may not seem traditional, I have had great success with them. My attitude and mood are better, and I check things off my list. One bonus tidbit I'd add is to fully understand what the word "opportunity" means. I made a commitment to avoid adding any extra work during various quarters of the year and when an opportunity for my business and brand came across my lap that didn't serve me, I politely declined. Not that the opportunity wasn't worth it (because it truly was), but simply because I have to stay grounded in what I set as my standard. I must make sure I'm not burning myself out and losing time on other goals I've set. I honestly believe, "what's for me, is for me," and those other things will come back around. It's ok to not do everything!

Save those superpowers.

DreamBuilding Reminders

Let's ride this wave together. *But first*

Stop comparing yourself to others: I recently shared a conversation with a colleague who complained about not living a life she feels she deserves. She went on to say that she can outwork any IG model on any day. As I laughed about this I had to graciously remind her that, "Everythang ain't what it seems." People, even those close to us, do a lot of finessing that we simply don't know about. The grass isn't always greener and you have no idea what people have to go through. Comparison is a trap and I'm working on illuminating the voices of women and their "real" rise to success stories.

Stop wasting time: Tomorrow is never, ever promised. Stop putting your dreams on the back burner. You're never going to be fully prepared, or have enough money, or wisdom. What happens if you keep pushing it back or putting it off and you never get a chance to execute? You literally have to start today.

Stop doubting your ability: You don't need fancy degrees to begin movements or to do the things you love. You need to know that fear is an ugly enemy that you can conquer. God will provide you with the strength of an army—things you could never imagine. Listen, if this little black girl from the West Side of Detroit did it, baby nothing is in your way!!!! Remember it's a continual process.

Don't be discouraged: Every single thing has already been done!!!! It's inevitable that you'll do something completely different. Your idea or dream may be an interpretation or a different version that someone else has publicly executed. That's OK. There isn't another YOU that exists and we need YOU to live your dream life. We need you to connect your passion and your purpose. We need your story, your style, and your imprint on the world. There is enough room for ALL of us to win. Don't ever feel like your idea isn't original (it probably isn't), but that's not what it's about. It's about the impact you make on others!!!!!!

The Dream Building Diary | your personal journey to creating and living the life of your dreams

Notes:

Chapter 5 Recap

Chapter 5: Execute the Dream/Experience the Outcomes	
Dream Brainstorm	A personal think tank to brain dump ideas, thoughts, concerns, or comments.
Project Identity Brainstorm	Branding Planning Sheet.
Build & Balance	Daily Task Management.
Monthly Plan & Prep	Create your monthly mantra, inspiration goals, self-care goals, and more.
30.60.90 day Goals	Set goals with intentional benchmark deadlines.
Quarterly Planning	Break down goals by quarter.
Yearly Goal Map	Big Picture planning.
Design Blueprint	Describe, sketch, doodle, or draw your design.
Launch Plan Example	How to Use a Launch Plan.
Launch Plan	Blueprint to putting action to your planning.
Launch Plan Checklist	Actionable checklist to help move tasks along.
Monthly Reflection	Taking a look back to move forward.
Win Journal	Reflect on wins and outcomes, assessing challenges and success.
Inspiration Station	Short Reads (Insights, Tips, etc.)
Notes	For you to create.

Notes:

Notes:

Notes:

Notes:

Notes:

Notes:

Notes:

___

___

___

___

___

___

___

Doodles:

Notes:

Doodles:

Notes:

Doodles:

Notes:

Doodles:

Doodles:

Doodles:

Doodles:

Doodles:

Doodles:

$$\frac{\text{PASSION} + \text{PURPOSE} + \text{POWER}}{\textit{DreamBuilder}}$$

A Word from the Author

Hello Dreamer,

My superpower is curating experiences and creating thought-organizing tools for others to build a life they see when they close their eyes.

I was born and raised in Detroit, Michigan, and I live a life I've always dreamed. I have great friends, a handsome husband, and a hungry desire to try new things (*that's my real power*).

When I'm not hosting a Dream Retreat or creating tools such as this workbook (*this is the 2nd edition*), you can find me working and serving in the youth development field. I'm a designer, and I'm fortunate enough to create cool stuff in that arena also.

I absolutely love spending time with my friends and family, traveling to new places, cooking new recipes, working out, planning adventures, binge-watching shows, and loving on my precious dog Bailey.

I'd especially love to hear from you. Shoot me an email & say Hi!

Sincerely,
Kiylise M. Lowe
Founder & Chief Dream Engineer

The Dream Building Company
info@thedreambuildingco.com
www.thedreambuildingco.com